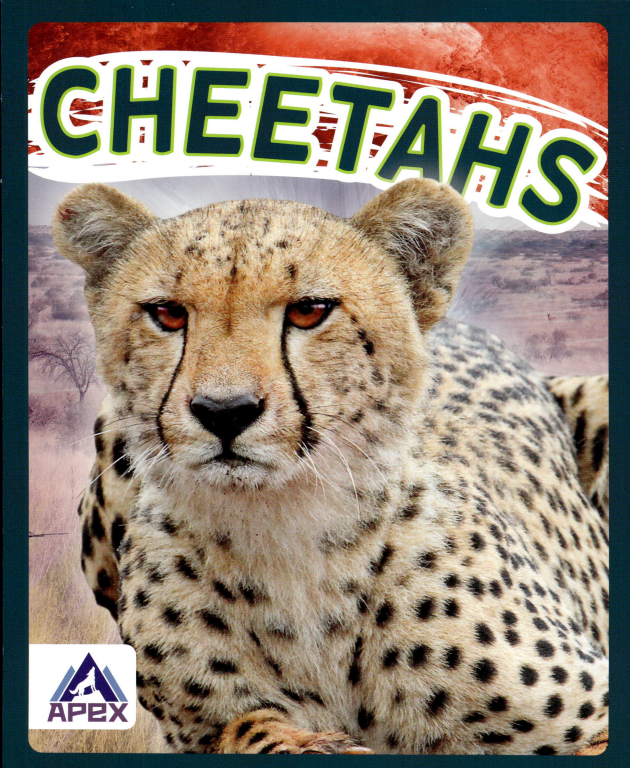

CHEETAHS

BY SOPHIE GEISTER-JONES

WWW.APEXEDITIONS.COM

Copyright © 2022 by Apex Editions, Mendota Heights, MN 55120. All rights reserved. No part of this book may be reproduced or utilized in any form or by any means without written permission from the publisher.

Apex is distributed by North Star Editions:
sales@northstareditions.com | 888-417-0195

Produced for Apex by Red Line Editorial.

Photographs ©: Shutterstock Images, cover, 1, 4–5, 6–7, 8–9, 12, 12–13, 14–15, 16–17, 19, 20–21, 22–23, 24–25, 25, 26–27, 29; iStockphoto, 10–11, 18

Library of Congress Control Number: 2020952939

ISBN
978-1-63738-028-4 (hardcover)
978-1-63738-064-2 (paperback)
978-1-63738-132-8 (ebook pdf)
978-1-63738-100-7 (hosted ebook)

Printed in the United States of America
Mankato, MN
082021

NOTE TO PARENTS AND EDUCATORS

Apex books are designed to build literacy skills in striving readers. Exciting, high-interest content attracts and holds readers' attention. The text is carefully leveled to allow students to achieve success quickly. Additional features, such as bolded glossary words for difficult terms, help build comprehension.

TABLE OF CONTENTS

CHAPTER 1
FAST FOOD 5

CHAPTER 2
LIFE IN THE WILD 11

CHAPTER 3
SPOTS AND STRIPES 17

CHAPTER 4
HOW CHEETAHS HUNT 23

Comprehension Questions • 28

Glossary • 30

To Learn More • 31

About the Author • 31

Index • 32

CHAPTER 1

FAST FOOD

A cheetah **crouches** in the long grass. An antelope **grazes** in front of her. It does not see her. The cheetah creeps slowly toward it. Then she **sprints** forward.

Cheetahs wait for animals to come close before running after them.

A cheetah can reach speeds of 70 miles per hour (113 km/h).

Cheetahs catch about half of the animals they chase.

The antelope tries to dash away. But it is too late. The cheetah is faster. She jumps onto the antelope's back. They both go down.

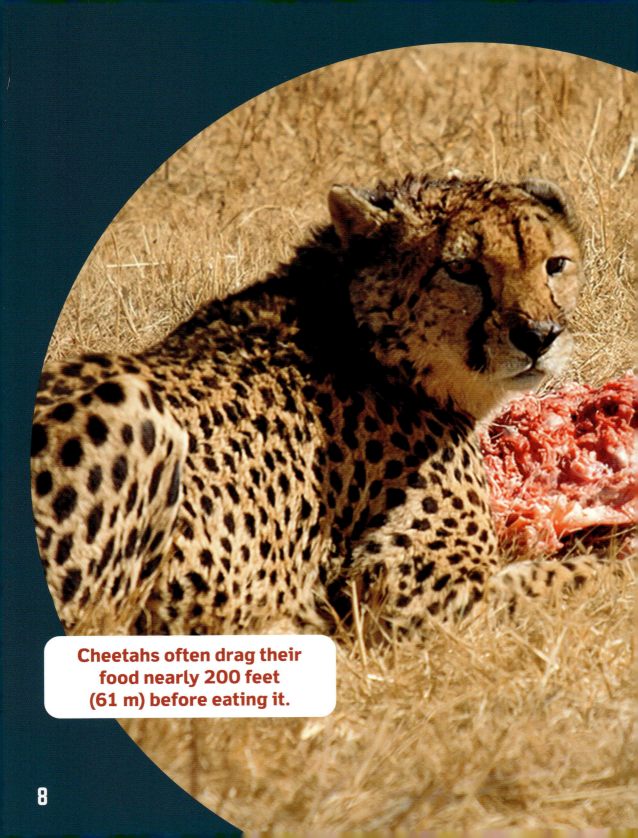

Cheetahs often drag their food nearly 200 feet (61 m) before eating it.

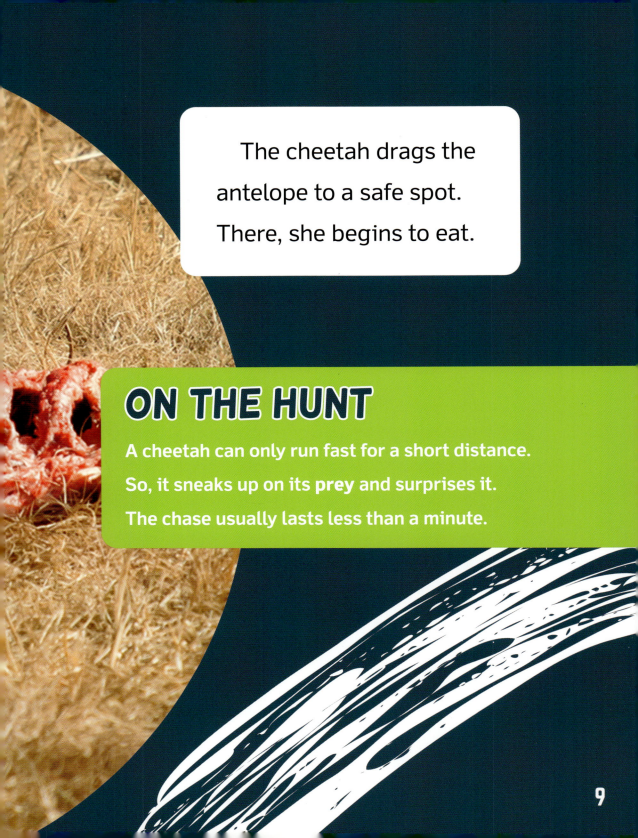

The cheetah drags the antelope to a safe spot. There, she begins to eat.

ON THE HUNT

A cheetah can only run fast for a short distance. So, it sneaks up on its **prey** and surprises it. The chase usually lasts less than a minute.

CHAPTER 2
LIFE IN THE WILD

Cheetahs live in Africa. They **roam** wide areas of land. Many cheetahs live in grasslands. But they can survive in plains and **deserts**, too.

The Serengeti Plain is a top place to see cheetahs.

When cheetahs are cubs, they live with their mother. She feeds them and teaches them to hunt. After about two years, the cubs can go live on their own.

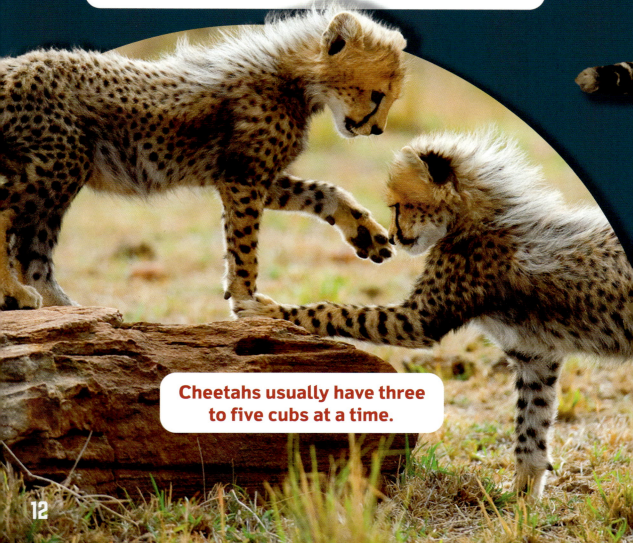

Cheetahs usually have three to five cubs at a time.

A mother cheetah often carries her cubs in her mouth.

CHEETAH CUBS

A mother cheetah keeps her cubs in a den. She goes out to hunt. Sometimes she brings live prey back to them. This helps the cubs practice hunting.

Female cheetahs live alone. Male cheetahs form small groups. Each group has two or three cheetahs. They live and hunt together.

Groups of cheetahs are called coalitions.

Unlike most big cats, cheetahs cannot roar. Instead, they bark, chirp, and purr.

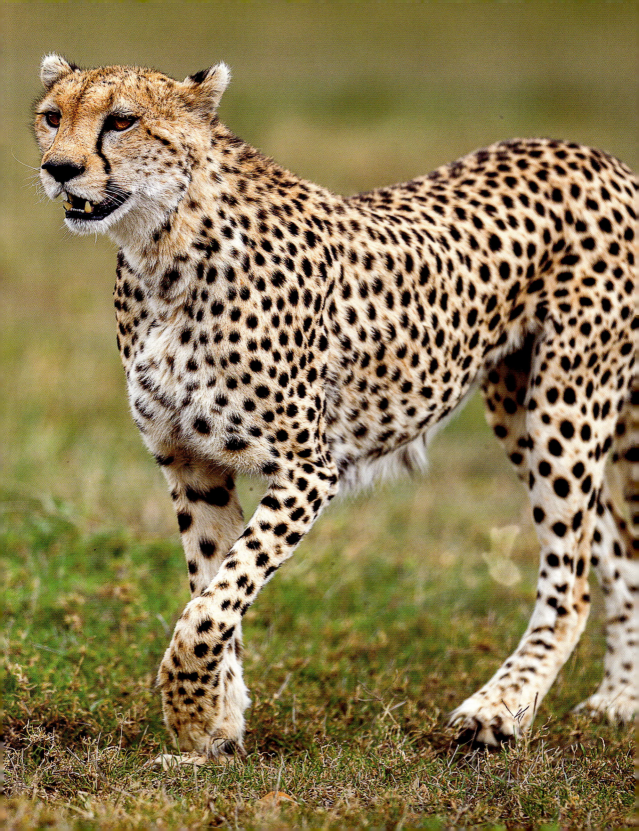

CHAPTER 3
SPOTS AND STRIPES

Cheetahs are big cats. They weigh between 75 and 140 pounds (34–64 kg). Male cheetahs tend to be larger than females.

A cheetah's tail can be 3 feet (1 m) long.

Cheetahs sometimes climb trees to look out over tall grasses.

Cheetahs are yellow with white bellies. They have spots all over. These markings help cheetahs blend in with the grass around them.

Black lines run from a cheetah's eyes to its mouth. They help block the sun's glare.

The black lines on a cheetah's face are called tear marks.

Cheetahs have thin bodies and long legs. This sleek shape helps them move very quickly.

A cheetah's legs are longer and thinner than the legs of most other big cats.

BUILT FOR SPEED

A cheetah's tail is almost as long as its body. A cheetah stretches out its tail when it runs. This helps the cat balance and turn quickly.

CHAPTER 4
HOW CHEETAHS HUNT

Cheetahs are excellent hunters. They can catch large animals. Cheetahs eat **gazelles** and **wildebeests**. Their diet also includes rabbits, birds, and warthogs.

Antelopes are a cheetah's main source of food.

Cheetahs do not see well in the dark. So, cheetahs hunt during the day. They often hunt in the morning or at **dusk**.

Cheetahs don't drink much water. They often go three or four days without drinking.

Cheetahs rest during the hot parts of the day.

A cheetah hunts wildebeests in Tanzania.

A cheetah bites an animal's neck to strangle it.

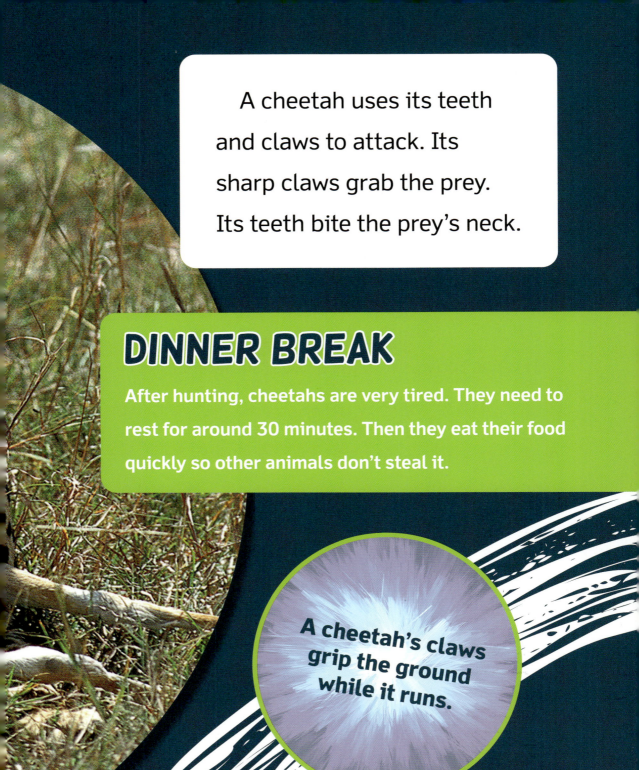

A cheetah uses its teeth and claws to attack. Its sharp claws grab the prey. Its teeth bite the prey's neck.

DINNER BREAK

After hunting, cheetahs are very tired. They need to rest for around 30 minutes. Then they eat their food quickly so other animals don't steal it.

A cheetah's claws grip the ground while it runs.

COMPREHENSION QUESTIONS

Write your answers on a separate piece of paper.

1. Write a sentence describing how cheetahs hunt their prey.

2. Would the place you live be a good home for a cheetah? Why or why not?

3. What body part helps a cheetah balance?

    A. its long tail
    B. its long legs
    C. its spotted fur

4. Why would bringing live prey to cubs help them learn to hunt?

    A. They could go far from the den.
    B. They could stay in the den forever.
    C. They could practice catching animals.

5. What does **diet** mean in this book?

*Cheetahs eat gazelles and wildebeests. Their **diet** also includes rabbits, birds, and warthogs.*

    A. where an animal lives
    B. what an animal eats
    C. what an animal sounds like

6. What does **sleek** mean in this book?

*Cheetahs have thin bodies and long legs. This **sleek** shape helps them move very quickly.*

    A. wide and short
    B. long and narrow
    C. big and heavy

Answer key on page 32.

GLOSSARY

crouches
Bends down and stays close to the ground.

deserts
Areas of land that have few plants and get very little rain.

dusk
The time of day just before night when the sky gets dark.

gazelles
Small antelopes that live in Africa and Asia. Most have thin bodies and long, curved horns.

glare
Very bright and strong light.

grazes
Eats grass or other plants growing in a field.

prey
An animal that is hunted and eaten by another animal.

roam
To move throughout a large area.

sprints
Runs very fast for a short period of time.

wildebeests
Large antelopes that live in Africa. They have long hair on their necks and short, curved horns.

TO LEARN MORE

BOOKS

Meinking, Mary. *Cheetahs*. Lake Elmo, MN: Focus Readers, 2018.

Olson, Elsie. *Animal Speed Showdown*. Minneapolis: Abdo Publishing, 2020.

Unwin, Cynthia. *Cheetahs*. New York: Scholastic, 2019.

ONLINE RESOURCES

Visit **www.apexeditions.com** to find links and resources related to this title.

ABOUT THE AUTHOR

Sophie Geister-Jones lives in Saint Paul, Minnesota. She loves reading. She and her brothers have a book club.

INDEX

A
antelope, 5, 7, 9

C
claws, 27
cubs, 12–13

D
den, 13
deserts, 11

G
gazelles, 23
grass, 5, 19
grasslands, 11
groups, 14

H
hunting, 12–14, 23–24, 27

L
legs, 20
lines, 19

P
plains, 11
prey, 9, 13, 27

R
resting, 27
running, 9, 21, 27

S
spots, 19

T
tail, 21
teeth, 27

W
water, 24
wildebeests, 23

Answer Key:
1. Answers will vary; **2.** Answers will vary; **3.** A; **4.** C; **5.** B; **6.** B